What's Happening to Morality?

By Nicholas Lohkamp, O

Nihil Obstat:
>Rev. Hilarion Kistner, O.F.M., S.T.D., S.S.L.
>Rev. John J. Jennings, S.T.D.

Imprimi Potest:
>Very Rev. Roger Huser, O.F.M.
>Provincial

Imprimatur:
>+Paul F. Leibold
>Archbishop of Cincinnati
>Feast of Mary, Mother of God
>January 1, 1971

The *Nihil Obstat* and *Imprimatur* are a declaration
that a book or pamphlet is considered to be free from
doctrinal or moral error. It is not implied that those
who have granted the *Nihil Obstat* and *Imprimatur*
agree with the contents, opinions, or statements
expressed.

Cover design by Lawrence Zink

SBN 0-912228-02-4
Library of Congress Catalog Card Number: 76-151400

Scripture quotations from *The New Testament in Modern English,* translated by J. B. Phillips, The Macmillan Company, ©J. B. Phillips, 1958

Contents

Introduction

everyone from Phyllis the hairdresser to the tycoons at Thorax, Inc., knows that "something" is happening to morality. It just isn't what it used to be.

Many are quite concerned: parents whose children are being taught religion "differently"; older people who feel that tried and true moral laws are being ignored by the young; pastors who try to hold the line and "lay down the law," yet find that few people pay attention.

Many people feel that the Church is doing more than "changing into modern garments." From their present vantage point (or disadvantage point), the dropping of Friday abstinence seems a relatively mild upset, after all. Now the teaching of Pope and Bishops, once accepted almost absolutely as the word of God, is questioned by some; and men who profess to be loyal and conscientious sons of the Church claim the right to dissent from all but infallible teaching. A sense of security in the "one true

Church" seems to be ebbing away.

Has the Church become too human? Will it maintain its God-given status if it tolerates "way-out" opinions within its fold; if it confesses its faults publicly in a Council; if it cooperates with "outsiders," even atheists; if it accepts "the world"?

And finally, the clincher: "Now you can follow your own conscience"—a statement that seems to be variously interpreted to mean: a) morality is a private affair; b) law is "out"; c) if you have a good reason, anything's good; d) you can do whatever you please.

Is it all that bad?

This books tries to show that it *isn't* all that bad. It will attempt to make clear what is good and exciting in the new emphases in moral theology. It will try to show that a challenge has arisen which will shake Christians to the roots of their lives, a demand that will not make life "easier" but will require a deep and total personal relationship with Christ.

The author hopes this book will make clear the beauty, the promise and the demands of the new emphasis, and that it will separate true fears from false, reassure those who fear the ship is going down, and make real and compelling the Good News Christ is proclaiming today.

ARTIN
E BISSET
N HEFLIN
NELSON
HOWARD
HELLO DOLLY
ARGENTINO
DANCE
AUTOMAT
Oh! Calcutta
to believe

Chapter I

What's

Happening to

Morality?

the only way to decide whether Joe World has changed or not is to look at what he *was.* Even more important is knowing what he *should* be, then and now.

Before we can discuss what is happening to morality, we should have a clear idea of exactly what we mean by the term. Next we should attempt to describe morality as it was generally presented in the past. Then we can identify some of the far-reaching changes that have occurred, particularly in man's view of God, man and the world.

What Is "Morality"?

Obeying a law may be morally good, but morality is much more than obeying or violating laws. Adultery is an immoral act, but immorality is much broader than sexual deviation. Morality is a *quality* that is present in every instance of truly human activity. This moral aspect is one of

1

goodness or badness. It is good for me to care for this sick person; it is bad for me to loaf on the job. And the reason I make this judgment is my conviction that what I do or don't do affects my relationship with God. That which promotes my relationship with God is good; that which hinders it is bad.

What is "moral" has to do with goodness or badness that I am now *aware of* and *freely decide* upon. Morality, therefore, is a *condition* or *quality* of my actions: they are good or bad because of what they are as my choices—not because of some extraneous influence like a clock that does not get me up for Sunday Mass. Morality is the *way* I respond to God and to other people, in view of all I know about God's love.

Now, in this sense, there is no "new" or "old" morality. There is just morality, a quality in our actions that comes from the fact that we are persons—conscious and free—who can accept or refuse God's coming to us.

This brings up the question: if morality has to do with what is good or bad in my relationship with God, how do we judge whether or not some word, thought, act or omission is in harmony with our relationship with God (and therefore "good") or hindering it (and therefore "bad")? This is a very complex question. It involves our whole understanding of God and His dealings with men, of man and what it means to be human. It involves our understanding of creation, incarnation, and redemption, of revelation, nature and grace, the Church, the world, and human society. Obviously we cannot here explore all these aspects. We can only give an oversimplified overall view of the way our question has generally been answered in the past, and a description of the kind of morality it fostered. Then we shall attempt to give a bird's-eye view of the present-day answer, and the morality it fosters. Then, hopefully, we shall have some idea of what's happening to morality.

The Worldview of the Past

In this view God is indeed the God of the Covenant, the God of Mercy; but predominantly He is the Supreme Lawgiver, the God of Sinai. In the New Testament, Jesus is the perfect lawgiver, who came "not to destroy but to fulfill" the law, who said: "If you love me, keep my commandments." Over the centuries, the Church came to be more or less identified with the hierarchy, and very special emphasis was given to the authority of the Pope and Bishops to teach all matters of faith and morality. The laity were expected to listen and obey.

Love was not lost sight of, indeed it was often greatly stressed, but when all was said and done, the greatest expression of love was to obey fully all the laws of God, Church and State. At the same time, because of the influence of Plato, Aristotle, and the philosophy of Scholasticism, the world and human nature were looked upon in an abstract and static way. Man's unchanging "essence," disentangled from

3

his changeable everyday "messing around," was sought as the really important matter.

In this view, man is a "rational animal," composed of "body" and "soul," living in a world of "substances" (wood-ness, man-ness) and "accidents" (color, length, age). In the world around him, and in his own nature and functions, man discovers the will of God who created all things as they are. Thus understood, human nature never changes and is the same in all men. Therefore, we can formulate absolute norms of morality which hold true for all men at all times.

In this view the answer to the question "How do we judge whether an action is morally good or bad?" is fairly simple. If it is not contrary to the law (of God, Church, state) as taught by the Church, then it is in harmony with our relationship to God; it is good. Hence, the main concern is with law, and with the violation of law. With such a preoccupation, the danger is a growing legalism (concern with the letter of the law to the detriment of its spirit) and forgetfulness of God as Person. A further danger is excessive preoccupation with sin: the major concern is "What are the ways in which law is violated?" There is a growing satisfaction with the minimum: "How far can I go without committing serious sin?" A further danger of such preoccupation with law is that Christian life is seen as "keeping the Commandments," with little concern for the rest of one's life; the perfection of the Christian life is left for nuns, brothers and priests.

This may seem to be an oversimplification of the way morality has been understood for centuries. Yet, anyone over 25 will remember the complicated rules surrounding the communion fast, what was allowed and not allowed on days of fast and/or abstinence, the detailed regulations about servile work on Sunday, the ways one could commit mortal or venial sins by missing parts of Sunday Mass, the many ways one could break the sixth and ninth commandments—and all the guilt feelings and scrupulosity this whole approach engendered.

Modern Worldview

God is understood by modern man not so much as Lawgiver "up there," but as incarnate, as immanent, as God with us. God becomes man! Redemption comes about through humanity. All creation, all men, find their meaning in terms of Christ. The "face" of God becomes visible in the face of Jesus, and so in every human face. All morality is understood in terms of our relationship to Christ. The stress is on the fact that we are members of Christ, that all are called to become sons and daughters of God in Christ, and that Christ has established a Kingdom which grows until His final coming.

This understanding of morality is drawn from Scripture with its predominant concern for Christ, vocation, conversion, faith-love, freedom and growth. It finds very congenial ideas in modern philosophy which stresses the person

5

(rather than abstract essences), the historical, time-and-space conditions of life (rather than the timeless and unchanging aspects), the dynamic, growing, maturing aspects of human existence (rather than the static).

The Church, too, is looked upon differently. She is no longer the predominantly monolithic teacher and lawgiver; she is now People of God, Pilgrim People, People of Covenant. Authority is less centralized; collegiality is stressed. No longer are the laity considered "sheep," children, a passive presence; now they are "Church," priestly, kingly, prophetic people, called as adults to share actively in the living and proclaiming of the Gospel. In this Church, Pope and Bishops are still divinely commissioned to teach, but not without listening closely to the laity in whose lives and experience the Spirit also dwells.

Perhaps we can say that in this modern worldview the ideas of person, personal freedom, growth, and personal responsibility reign supreme. God has created a world, but only in outline; it is an evolving world, and man's is the task of mastering, guiding, and ruling it as it evolves. God has created man in the image and likeness of Christ, as person. Each human person is called to freedom and self-realization, which are not "given," but are tasks to be pursued in an evolving world and in community with other persons.

The primary emphasis is not on God, or Church, as lawgiver. Laws have their place, but it is decidedly a secondary place. God has created for man an evolving world of time and space, filled with innumerable things and plants and animals; but above all with unimaginable potentialities. God has given existence to human persons, called them to sonship in Christ, and given them the summons to become *adult* and human persons, living together in love, and working together to better human conditions and create a better world.

In this modern worldview, God is not seen as "out there." He is incarnate; He is present in the world, in every human event, in every human person. He is present as one who calls men to ever greater self-actualization, freedom, maturity; to ever greater and deeper communion with one another. God is present not so much as the lawgiver who holds men responsible for observing or violating laws, but as one who makes man responsible for himself, for others, for the whole world, for the whole moral order.

In such a worldview, love and loving concern for persons becomes the supreme value (to love human persons is to love Christ); personal growth in freedom and loving communion with other persons is the supreme goal. Consequently, there is great concern for the personal, the unique, the concrete, the existential, the historical, the ever present fact of change. There is less concern for particular laws, even universal laws, especially when these do not seem to be based on an understandable rationale, and most especially when these seem to interfere with personal growth, and forbid what seems to be the loving response in a given situation. Finally, this worldview lays great stress on the uniqueness of the person and the unrepeatable aspects of his concrete situations, aspects which no law can embrace. All this—when understood in the light of the overriding norm: "Act responsibly, do the most loving thing for the most people"—helps us see why there is a "new morality."

Checking the Record

Perhaps this oversimplified description of two different worldviews, or starting points, will help explain what's happening to morality. Does all this mean that the moral fibre of those who espouse the modern worldview is deteriorating, or has totally rotted away? Are those who follow the new morality irresponsible? Are people today—especially young people—more immoral than people in the past? These and many other questions grow out of a genuine concern of many for the moral order. In reflecting on such questions it is important that we try to be honest and look at the facts.

Most of us older people cannot really be too proud of our own moral growth and performance in the past. Many, if not most of us, are quite concerned about obedience to laws; yet we have been far from outstanding in our love for one another, the most important law of all. Most of us are quite concerned about distractions in prayer and Sunday Mass, but apparently not so concerned about showing genuine love and respect and care for our neighbors, especially if

10

they are black or of a "lower" class. Most of us are quite alarmed at the sexual abuses of the young on college campuses, but perhaps too ready to shut our eyes to the horrors of war, poverty, starvation and racial injustice.

On the other hand, who are the ones clamoring for peace and the end of war, fighting for racial justice, standing up for the dignity and rights of every human person? Who are the ones stressing authenticity and maturity, proclaiming the primacy of loving concern for persons, and human community? These are above all people who follow the new morality. They may be guilty of abuses, and excessive disregard for law and authority may be their weakness; but the facts seem to indicate reasons for hope.

This hope that the new morality will gradually bring about genuine moral development (and *not* deterioration) rests chiefly on the values stressed: person, freedom, love, community, peace (all of which are strongly emphasized in Scripture). These values, together with a stress on sincerity, openness, authenticity, growth, and a preoccupation with the uniqueness of the existential situation and the ever present fact of change in our society and the world—all these seem to offer reasonable basis for the hope that morality is changing for the better.

The reason for hope is supported by what Vatican II has said about morality. It declared that morality must be renewed and perfected, much more profoundly based on Sacred Scripture. This means that the basic orientation of morality will derive from our Christian vocation (the personal call of the Father and our personal response—all in Christ). Flowing from this vocation, morality will be concerned above all with our obligation to live in love, a love that will effectively bear fruit in promoting life and community among our fellow men. The rest of this book will be an attempt to expand further these very ideas of Vatican II.

What we have indicated above about the new morality seems to harmonize with the strong statements of Vatican II concerning the nature of the Church, the role of the Church in the modern world, and the necessary renewal of morality.

That there *is* a new morality seems quite obvious from the way people are living. That those who seek to follow the new morality are irresponsible and altogether selfish seems an entirely unwarranted assumption. That those who follow the new morality are making mistakes, even sinning at times may well be true, but that proves nothing about the new morality itself. Those who follow the old morality are sinners too! That the new morality is risky, demands much greater personal responsibility, and provides much less security seems also quite evident and is perhaps the strongest argument in its favor.

One thing seems quite certain: morality will never be the same as it was. Hopefully, what is happening in morality, the new morality, will enable us to become more fully human, more fully Christian. Following the ideas of Vatican II, we will now explore the reasons for this hope.

Questions for Discussion

1. How are you aware of your personal relationship to God?

2. What is necessary that an act or attitude be morally good or bad?

3. What is the difference between legalism and respect for law?

4. What key words help you express the emphases of the new morality?

5. What is the principal "image" of God in the new morality? of man? of the world?

Chapter II

The
Christ-Centered
Vocation of
Christians

the bishops of Vatican II call upon moral theologians to shed light on the lofty *vocation* of the Christian—every Christian—*in Christ. All* the faithful are called by the Father, in Christ, to bear fruit in love for the life of the world. Here we have the heart of moral theology, and the aspect that is being most vigorously explored in the new morality.

Today Christian morality stresses that it's not enough for John Brown and Mary Smith to be baptized and try to avoid sin. It's not enough to keep the commandments. Their vocation is to live Christ, to "put on" Christ, to *become* more and more Christian. Whether as lumberjack or housewife, lawyer or actress, John Brown and Mary Smith are called to live the whole of their daily lives so as to grow up in all things like Christ.

It is *Christ* who is our way, our truth, and our life. We Christians are called to follow the *way of this God-man Jesus.* Two magnificent chapters in St. Paul (Ephesians 1 and Colossians 1) are concerned with this one central and tremendous thought, that Christ is the Beginning and the End. He is all in all.

The "new" morality stresses above all that we become *Christian* from head to toe, from morning till night. Mary Smith, whether she spends her life washing dishes or teaching school or editing a fashion magazine, is called to do so in a certain way, with a certain spirit—as a Christian. John Brown, whether at work, at home, with wife or children or friends, is called to be *different* because he is alive in Christ and Christ lives in him. He will be different especially because his attitudes, his disposition, his orientation toward people and things that fill his life are different. He is *Christian*; he seeks really to allow Christ to be his way, truth and life.

It is not as though Christ were a sort of static model fixed forever on a wall, so that we might look at Him occasionally and then go imitate Him. "Let this *mind* be in you, which was in Christ Jesus." We must *live* Christ. He is not a model outside ourselves. We do not merely repeat what He did (like one of the simple followers of St. Francis, who blithely did whatever the saint did: knelt, coughed, folded his hands, closed his eyes, scratched his ear). The power whereby we live and act is His power; the reasons we do things are His reasons; the Spirit that energizes us is His Spirit; the love that we express to God and man is His love—not in external imitation, but in a union of life.

16

When we think about this: "I have been *called*—called *by name*" we already have a revelation of God's love and mercy, because it is "I, a sinner" who have been called. The fact that He has called me, in Christ, to live His kind of life, to live Christ—it is an overwhelming thought.

People receive many "calls" in their lives. Mary is "called" to play the lead role in a play. Jim is "called" to serve his country. One "call" we often receive is an invitation to share a pleasant evening with friends. Far beyond any such "calls" is the call we receive from God, a call to share His very life, to become His son or daughter, to come alive in Christ.

We would treasure a similar kind of call from Pope or President, and respond to it energetically. Here it is God Himself who calls each of us personally. This is the overwhelming *fact* of our Christian existence.

This call is *gift*. This vocation is *grace*. The invitation is actualizing grace, and the response brings about personal union with God in Christ—divinizing grace. God loved us first, and called us when we were sinners. The Father reconciles us to Himself in Jesus. He calls us with a personal call, to live as fully as possible the life of Jesus. It is a personal call to me in all my uniqueness, in accordance with my own status and position in life, suited exactly to the capacities God has given me.

This concept of vocation—calling—is fundamental throughout the whole history of God's dealing with man. At least here are people I can relate to. Abraham, "our father in faith," was called; Israel was chosen, called, by God; the prophets were called; Mary, the apostles—*every* Christian. And so Paul can say in Ephesians: "Walk in a manner worthy of your calling!"

This call is a *love* call and it demands a response. It is a challenge that cannot be ignored. We can say Yes or No, but we cannot remain indifferent. There must be a response of one kind or another.

Vocation

It is here that we get into the notion of morality as responsibility. God gives us responsibility. He has given us existence, brought us to life in Christ. He has given us intelligence, the capacity to discern value. He has given us freedom, the capacity to determine ourselves in response to value. He has given us the Spirit to guide us in our response to others. In short, God has equipped us for a task, *made us responsible*.

Our responsibility involves our whole stance in the world, our whole commitment to fostering values, especially the good of persons. Our one great imperative is: act responsibly! The world is the place in which we are to do God's work. Our every act is a religious act because everything we do for human persons we do for Christ. In all our human experience, in all human events, we act so as to promote the growth of persons and human community. Thus do we act responsibly, and fulfill our vocation.

Here is Mike, husband and father of five,

ironworker in South Chicago, fiery and restless by temperament. He seeks to give his response not only in terms of who he is, but also in terms of his status as husband, father, ironworker. He seeks to give his daily response not *in spite* of his circumstances and situation but precisely in and through all of them.

Above all, my response extends to *the giving of my whole self*, not just a little time here and there, an occasional relationship that can be terminated in favor of other things. God wants our hearts, our thoughts, our feelings, as well as our actions. "I will be your God: you will be my people."

My prayer at noon, my sympathy for another in the evening, my patience with another at work, my Sunday Mass are not isolated cases of morality in my life. They are evidence of one spirit, expressions of my response, in all circumstances.

It is not that God has something all planned out for us to do. He wants the response that we are capable of in every moment. Jack, Ken, Pat, Karen each has intelligence and freedom, talents, gifts, capabilities. Each—in his or her own uniqueness—is called by God to fashion a response of love flowing from the heart of each, and embedded and enfleshed in all the circumstances of their lives.

The Many Ways

Our response to God has many facets. It is a *religious* response, for we are, in all our actions,

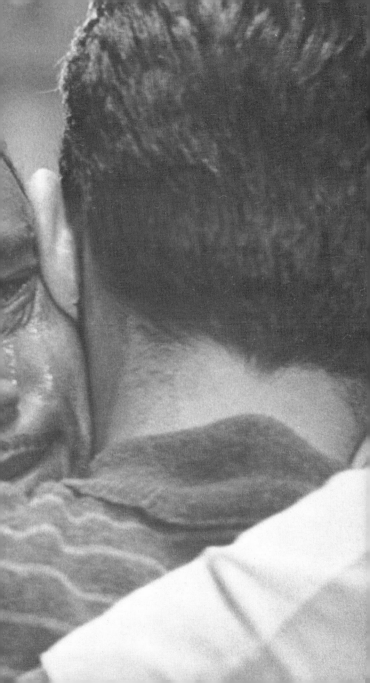

responsible to God; that is, we are recognizing Him, worshiping Him, trying to acknowledge Him, seeking to do His will.

Further, we should respond, not as isolated individuals, but as members of *Christ's community*. Hence our response is *ecclesial*, of the Church; we respond as one of the many brothers and sisters who are alive in Christ.

Thirdly, our response is *sacramental*. It goes back to that first moment when we were plunged into the dying and rising of Jesus in our baptism. This was the moment we came alive in Christ and were given the capacity to believe and hope and love. This initial moment is to be carried out and confirmed in our daily life, deepened, increased and extended.

Fourthly our response to God must be *"spiritual"*; that is, we are led by the Spirit of Jesus in giving our wholehearted response. The Holy Spirit lives in us precisely to refashion us in the image of Christ, enlightening and encouraging us so that we *will* allow Christ to live in us and we in Him.

Finally, our response ought always to be a *dynamic* one. It is never finished and done with; it is always reaching and growing. It is not content to look to the past and be satisfied. The Christian is always straining ahead. He is a pilgrim and stranger on the move, involved in continual conversion: recognizing and being sorry for all the obstacles he places to the grace of the Spirit, always trying to grow. Stagnation, and complacency are enemies of the spirit.

The Response Is a Loving Response

Vatican II insisted that morality has to do with the vocation of all Christians to bring forth fruit in love. The response of the Christian is a loving response. The call is a love call, and the response must be a love answer. To live God's kind of life, to live in Christ, to be led by the Spirit is to respond in love.

Christian morality must start with the fundamental statement of Christ. "Master, which is the greatest commandment of the Law?" Jesus said, "You must love the Lord your God with all your heart, with all your soul, and with all your mind. This is the greatest and the first commandment." So, the martyr who pours out his blood, the missionary who spends his life spreading the Gospel, the husband and wife, the teacher and social worker—every person who believes in God and tries to give himself or herself daily and ever more completely is really living this greatest commandment. "The second resembles it: You must love your neighbor as yourself. On these two commandments depend the whole law, and the Prophets also" (Mt. 22:36-40).

In the Sermon on the Mount, Christ made very clear the inescapable bond between love of God and love of neighbor. You cannot love God unless you love your neighbor—your brother, taken concretely—this very person, right here before you. "Your neighbor" taken absolutely—no limits, exceptions. This demand of Christian morality is therefore the standard of God's judgment: "I was hungry and you gave me to eat" (Mt. 25:35). The criterion of how we loved Him is how we have loved one another.

Christ did not merely "talk" this morality. He showed it in the actions of His life. The whole mystery of the incarnation, death and resurrection is His actual loving of His brothers.

He loved and delivered Himself up for us. To share in His life is to share in this dying and rising. The vocation of the Christian is to be and to *live* as a son of the Father, in Christ. The Christian "puts on" Christ in adoring love for the Father and in serving love for his brothers and sisters. We must literally lay down our lives for the brethren as Christ did!

Again, this actual fruitfulness of a Christian's life is possible only if he is led by the Spirit. "Since the Spirit is our life," St. Paul says, "let us be directed by the Spirit. When self-indulgence is at work, the results are obvious . . . But what the Spirit brings is very different: love, joy, peace, patience, kindness, goodness, trustfulness, gentleness and self-control" (Gal. 5:22).

Or, as St. John records of Christ: "Whoever remains in Me, with Me in Him, bears fruit in plenty . . . You did not choose me, but I chose you, to go out and bear fruit, fruit that will last" (Jn. 15:5 & 16).

For the World

Finally, the Council Fathers stressed the fact

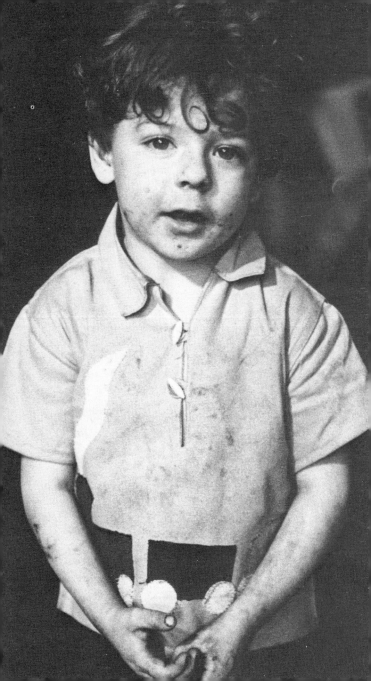

that morality has to do with the Christian life, bearing fruit in charity, must do so *for the life of the world*. Here we have the social and apostolic dimension of Christian morality. We are called to live for others. To be alive in Christ is to share in the mission of Christ to the world. His mission is ours: to bring the Good News, to share the wealth of God's self-revealing, to bring God's call to holiness and salvation to all men.

Christ said, "My flesh is food for the *life of the world*" (John 6:51). The Christian must bear fruit for the life of the world. Christian morality, if it is to deserve the name, must be oriented to the world. To be truly Christian, it must have a social dimension.

Social Morality

Consequently, morality has a two-fold dimension—personal and social. Society depends very much on personal morality, and personal morality influences society in many and deep ways. Bearing fruit for the life of the world demands that we work positively to protect and augment *our own life in Christ* first of all. But our concern for the world is bound up with our own personal response to God in Christ. It is not something we can take or leave, but a serious obligation for all of us.

"Go, live the Mass" means "Go and bring Christ to the *world*." This means that Christ is somehow being expressed in our life.

The Council says, "The faithful must learn the deepest meaning and value of all creation, and how to relate it to the praise of God. By their competence in secular fields and by their personal activity, elevated from within by the grace of Christ, let them work vigorously so that by human labor, technical skill and civic culture, created goods may be perfected for the benefit of every last man ... Through the members of his Church Christ will progressively illumine the whole of human society with his saving light" *(Constitution of the Church*, No. 36).

Questions for Discussion

1. What should be the most obvious fact about being "Christian"?

2. What precisely does Christ share with us, so that we are Christian?

3. If we have a vocation, or call, what are we called *to*?

4. Is morality the same as responsibility?

5. What strikes you as the most important characteristic of Christian response?

6. What can be said of the accusation that social concern is "politics" and has nothing to do with "religion"?

Chapter III

The Nobility of The Christian Vocation

highborn" is not a word that fits easily into the American vocabulary. We tend to feel that no one is "noble-by-birth," but rather should prove his worth and make his own mark in life.

Perhaps that is why we have difficulty understanding one of the fundamental facts of our Christian life: by God's grace, we who were sinners have been given a new existence that truly makes us noble in His sight. It is this fact of Christian dignity and God-given personal value that underlies almost everything that is to be said about Christian morality.

The bishops of Vatican II urged that this Christian nobility be stressed in the renewal of moral theology. In our present discussion, it is time to see how this can be done.

God our Father, Paul tells us, chose us before the world was made. He chose us, in Christ, to become His holy and blameless children, living within His constant care. He planned that we should be adopted as His own children through Christ.

This is the *fact* of our Christian vocation in Christ. The *nobility* lies in our having been called by the Father himself through His very own Spirit, in Christ. We are called to share a life that is fully human, yet more than human; we are called to share in God's life. For a migrant worker to share the life of a President of the United States would be a great gift. For us to share God's life is immeasurably greater.

God has no need of us. There is nothing we can contribute to Him. Yet, in the mystery of His love, He wants us; His love goes out 'to us; and in that sense He "needs" us. Love is the life of God that pours itself out within the Trinity. Somehow God wants to join men together in a similar community of love: a community of persons in Christ, a people who will worship Him by responding to His love.

This God loves each of us personally. He calls each one of us by name. We have experienced being called by name in many ways: by a teacher, by an employer, by an acquaintance. But there is nothing so moving or compelling as to be called by name by a friend who loves us deeply. This is like being called by God. His call is a summons to the very core of our person.

Even more amazing is the fact that He loves us and calls us who are sinners. The very purpose of His call is to bring men, who are sinners, into life and community. His call is a call to salvation. All of Scripture describes how God the Father takes the initiative of merciful and faithful love toward His prodigal children. Scripture is the history of salvation, a history of at-one-ment: oneness with God.

He *first* loved us, and delivered Himself up for us. As St. Paul says in Romans, it is impossible to imagine a man laying down his life for another man—though one might possibly do it for a good man. But the amazing thing about God's love is that Jesus laid down His life for us when we were sinners. We begin to understand how precious this call to life in Christ really is.

Such an ennobling vocation is *gift*. But it is also challenge. If the gift is so great, conferring such nobility, then the demand for a response is equally great. The challenge of our Christian life begins to sink in when we realize that we have been called *by name* personally, to live a life that is as fully as possible a response to divine love.

There is no better way to consider this challenge than to hear the words of Jesus Himself, as He began His public life: "The time has come, at last. The kingdom of God has arrived. You must change your hearts and minds and believe in the Good News" (Mark 1:15). In a sense these stirring words sum up the whole of Christ's revelation. The time is now, the kingdom of God is here and now in the person of Jesus. The challenge is to respond by changing totally our hearts and minds and believe in the Good News of Christ. The urgency of this challenge is clear in the Bible: "God, who gave to our forefathers many different glimpses of the truth in the words of the prophets, has *now* at the end of the present age, given us the truth in his Son" (Hebrews 1). "The present time is of the highest importance" (Rom. 13:11). "*Now* is the acceptable time, and this very day is the day of salvation" (II Cor. 6:2). The time has come at last. The Kingdom of God has arrived.

Penance

Changing one's mind and heart—which is the "penance" Christ spoke of—is a crucial challenge, for it involves a changing of our whole selves. It means turning away from our former paths, striking out in a new direction. It has to do with our very attitude, all our human powers. It is a seeking to turn away from, and to atone for, our sinfulness, for all the obstacles in ourselves to the coming of God's kingdom. It means "putting on the *new* man, which has been created according to God in justice and holiness of truth" (Eph. 4:24).

But, though repentance involves very much the awareness that we are sinners, it brings an even greater awareness that our Father is a merciful Father and Jesus a merciful savior. There is a keen and honest realization of our sinfulness, our weakness, our selfishness, and we don't try to excuse these.

But our sinfulness does not overwhelm us for we see it in the light of God's mercy and call to salvation. It is by the very favor of His call that we are enabled to admit our sinfulness and turn to Him for mercy and judgment, believing in Him, and confident of His love. The parable of the Prodigal Son is a vivid manifestation of repentance on man's part, and even more of the merciful love of the Father.

Faith

Jesus then goes on to say, "You must *believe* in the Good News." Here the emphasis is on faith. In "change your mind and heart" the emphasis is on conversion, what happens in *us*; whereas, believing in the Good News is going out of ourselves, believing in the merciful love and call of the Father. Faith, here, welcomes the Good News that the Father loves us and sends His Son, that Jesus loves us and delivers Himself up for us. We come to *believe* in this kind of love.

Because we can come to the Father only through Christ, our faith is centered in Jesus. Jesus is "the Good News." Through Him the Father is establishing within men's hearts the royal rule of His kingdom. We seek to have "that mind in us which was in Christ Jesus." We seek to accept the person of Jesus in His Godhead and in His humanness, and to obey Him through whom the Father communicates His will to us. It is only insofar as we come to accept the *person* of Jesus that we will come to have faith in the *message* of Jesus. We will then come to accept His words and His deeds, not in a detached and uncommitted way, but as positvely as we

33

can, and with all the awareness of the consequences.

Believing in the Good News is something
that begins and grows in the Christian. Faith becomes a real bond between oneself and God,
involving one in holding fast the words of Jesus
and in seeking to take refuge in the powerful,
creative and redeeming love of Jesus. As Paul
puts it in Chapter Four of Romans, all
Christianity is a matter of faith on man's part,
generosity and goodness on God's part. God
gives the security of His own promise to all men
who can be called the children of Abraham, that
is, both those who have lived in faith by the Law
and those who have shown a faith like that of
Abraham. As John says, "This is eternal life, to
believe in Jesus." So, as Jesus proclaimed, the
time has come at last, the kingdom of God has
arrived. The challenge before us is to change our
minds and hearts and to believe in the Good
News. This is how we respond to the nobility of
our vocation . . .

"Follow Me"

The response to this proclamation of Jesus
demands *discipleship*. To believe in Jesus is to
accept His invitation and demand: "Follow me."
To be a Christian is to be a disciple of Christ.
But, to follow Christ, to be His disciple, is far
more than imitating some of His external activities. Our very being in Christ is the source of
discipleship. As Christ Himself said, "I am the
vine and you are the branches. Without Me you

do not even have life" (John 15:5). Only insofar as you abide in Me and I in you are you alive. Being, that is living in Christ, is the source of our ability to live and act as disciples. St. Paul tries to express the same thing by using the analogy of the human body: we are living members of Christ; we live with His life (I Corinthians, ch. 12). Again he says, "The secret is simply this: Christ in you" (Colossians 1:27). This happens originally in baptism. But this union with Christ is to become deeper and more pervasive as we grow.

The expression of this discipleship is guided by one principle: *Christ* becomes the law of my life. There is more involved here than just a teacher-pupil relationship. It is more than knowing what somebody (in this case Jesus) taught, then heeding it, appreciating it, and somehow trying to let it influence our life. Christ as the law of our life demands a radical change in our life, a whole new way of living.

This radical change is described very concretely in the Sermon on the Mount. The disciple is to become humble-minded, poor in spirit, if the kingdom of God is to be his. He is to be one who knows what sorrow means because the Jesus whom he follows is a crucified Jesus. The disciple of Jesus is one who claims nothing, who hungers and thirsts for goodness and holiness, is full of mercy, is utterly sincere, a peacemaker, one who suffers persecution. This is the cost of discipleship.

Or as Jesus sums it up, "If anyone wants to

follow in My footsteps, he must give up all rights to himself, carry his cross every day and keep close behind Me" (Luke 9:21). And elsewhere, "A grain of wheat has to fall to the ground and die or it remains itself alone, but if it dies it can bring forth fruit" (John 12:24).

The Characteristics of Discipleship

Discipleship means being led by the Spirit. In Ezekiel 36, God foretells that in the New Covenant He is going to place His Spirit within man. In John's gospel several times Jesus promises to send the Spirit. He will be in us, teach us all that Jesus Himself commands us, and enable us to conform to Christ. Paul says, "You cannot even indeed be a Christian at all unless you have something of His Spirit in you, and all who follow the leading of God's Spirit are God's own sons" (Romans 8:9). In Galatians 5 Paul has much to say about living in the spirit and being led by the Spirit. "Live your whole life in the Spirit, and you will not satisfy the desires of your lower nature. If you follow the leading of the Spirit you stand clear of the Law. The Spirit produces in human life fruits such as these: love, joy, peace, patience, kindness, generosity, fidelity, tolerance, self-control. And there is no law against any of these. Those who belong to Christ Jesus have crucified their old nature and all that it loves. If our lives are centered in the Spirit, let us be guided by the Spirit."

Anyone of us knows that if these fruits of the Spirit are to be found in our own lives, there

will have to be a lot of changing done, and growing. We will need, above all, to be attentive to
the Spirit. We must be generous and unselfish in
following the promptings of the Spirit. This is
one of the reasons why prayer is such a
necessary demand in Christian life.

Now let us look at some particular characteristics of discipleship—qualities which the disciple
must allow to grow in him.

Free

The disciple is characterized as one who
seeks to follow Christ *from within*. He doesn't
just do certain things because someone tells him
to, or because there's a law. He is aware that
Christ is living in him and that the Spirit of Jesus
is prompting him to act, to think, to feel, so as
to conform to Christ. Christ is not outside of
him; He is within his being. The disciple lives
from within. Life comes from a center. "I live,
now not I, but Christ lives in me" (Gal. 2:20).

So Christ is *the* "law" of our life. All our
moral and religious imperatives flow from this:
put on the Lord Jesus Christ; live in Christ. Ours
is a life to be lived, not a set of rules to be
followed. And these—the laws of Church and
state—are seen in terms of this law of Christ, the
life we share in Him. The disciple then is one
who *wants* to follow Christ. It is this desire and
determination that directs our thoughts and
acts.

Personal

The disciple's response is also uniquely personal. We are indeed called to be members of a community. But the Father loves and calls each of us personally, by name, in Christ. The disciple of Christ is one who is struck by the personal relationship to which the Father is calling him, and his personal relationship with Christ, with the Holy Spirit. This is what makes all the difference in the way he looks on other people, at the world, at whatever happens in his life.

Dynamic

The disciple is characterized as one whose life is dynamic. Our life in Christ begins in baptism. But we can't stress enough that this is only the beginning. At no time in our life can we settle down, coast, or think we have "made it." We must be ever on the move, growing in Christ. We would consider a 21-year-old person deformed and stunted if he acted like a six-year-old. So also, as we mature as human beings, we ought to be growing up more and more as Christians. At 30 we ought to be following Christ in a different and more perfect way than we were at 15. Our life is to be one of continual conversion: a continual growth in putting on Christ's attitude; continual growth in our endeavor to do the will of the Father with Him; continual growth in being led by the Spirit. This characteristic is described by St. Paul: "Now I long to know Christ, and the power shown by his resurrection. I long to share his sufferings, even to die as he died, so that I may perhaps attain as he did the resurrection from the dead.

JESUS

Christ
had
promised
to those
who get
involved

LORD
end of my call
LORD
ve mercy.
l is longing
glory of
YOU

that they
will be
un be-
liever by
HAPPY
never
overcome
y TEAR
nd a
vays

Yet, my brothers, I do not consider myself as to have arrived spiritually, nor do I consider myself already perfect. But I keep going on, grasping ever more firmly that purpose for which Christ Jesus grasped me. My brothers, I do not consider myself to have fully grasped it even now, but I do concentrate on this: I leave the past behind, and with hands outstretched to whatever lies ahead I go straight for the goal" (Phil. 3:9-14).

Communitarian

The life of the disciple is a communitarian life. Salvation never comes to us in isolation, but precisely as members of God's people. Unique and individual as our life is, it is at the same time a life in community. We are our brothers' keepers—otherwise we cannot dare to say *our* Father. As Paul says, we must bear one another's burdens, because that is the way we fulfill the law of Christ.

Sacramental

Finally, the disciple's life is sacramental. Vatican II has reminded us that the liturgy, especially the Eucharist, is the source of all Christian activity. It is the culmination of worship and service. We are marked as being committed to the Christ life. The rest of our life as Christians is to be a flowering of what happened at Baptism and was confirmed by the Spirit in Confirmation. This commitment is to find expression in the celebration of the Eucharist, consecrating us for a life of worship culminating in union with God and for a life of service to our brothers.

It is in the awareness of the nobility of his vocation that the Christian senses the deep and obliging character of Paul's words: "Walk (*live*) in a manner worthy of your calling" (Eph. 4:1).

Questions for Discussion

1. What do you mean by the "dignity" of being a Christian?

2. In what ways has God taken the initiative in loving you?

3. Do we have faith in someone or something, or both?

4. What is the "radical" change required for discipleship of Christ?

5. If a disciple's attitude is characterized by being free, dynamic, sacramental and devoted to community, what are the opposing and unwholesome tendencies?

Chapter IV

The Supreme

Challenge:

Prudence

the new morality insists that all morality means responsibility. Therefore, the ever-present question that faces the Christian in every situation is "How am I to act *here and now* so as to be truly responsive to the will of God?"

There are guidelines for our response in Scripture and in the teaching of the Church. But these guidelines are quite general and certainly do not give us all the answers. At times they tell us what we may *not* do, but always there is the question that faces us in every situation and at every moment: What ought I do? Love, for example, demands that I do not hurt. But how am I to *love* in the here-and-now this particular person? The law forbids me to injure my health. What does that have to do with the fact that I am now smoking this cigarette, that I am now driving this automobile? It is precisely in this here-and-now that the kingdom of God *is at hand*, asking for a concrete response. How shall

I, considering who I am, respond?

This is the question of prudence, a much underestimated virtue that somehow has been relegated to such pale company as fainthearted-ness and excessive caution. ("Don't rock the boat," "Don't say anything, do anything, or change anything," and "Play it safe.") Actually, prudence is involved in both "playing it safe" and "taking a chance." It decides when each is the right thing to do. Prudence seeks to recognize the claim of God on me in the *here and now*. How am I to respond in *this* situation so as to be a true disciple of Christ?

The first requisite of prudence is *knowledge*. We must progressively understand who we are, what it means to be human both as individuals and as persons-in-relation. We must grow in the understanding of life in all its ramifications, in our family, in our work, in society at large. Even more important, we must grow in our knowledge of what it means to be Christian, to live in Christ.

Such knowledge involves a general awareness of moral doctrine. In the gradual acquisition of this background in moral doctrine and principles we are guided by our intelligence, by the wisdom of other persons, the teaching of the Church, and the revelation of God's word. In this way we come to appreciate such values as life, fidelity, justice, compassion, honesty, courage, truthfulness, gratitude, etc. We come to know in *general* how we should act to be disciples of Christ.

The Concrete Here and Now

We know, for example, that we must live so as to worship and give glory to God, so that whether we eat or drink or do anything else we do all to the glory of God. We know we must love our neighbor as Jesus loved us. We know that we must serve our brothers whoever they are, wherever we find them, whether they are worthy of it or not. We must love our enemies. We must be kind and thoughtful and helpful. We must be truthful and honest.

The wisdom of men and the teaching of the Church and the word of God help us by providing *general* guidelines and principles. But even with all this kind of knowledge and appreciation of moral values, there always remains the crucial question: "How do I bring this knowledge to bear in my concrete situation *here and now*? How am I to know what *is* the loving thing to do with regard to Joe Smith, 16-year-old drug addict about whom no one seems to care? How am I to know what is the honest thing to do, here and now, when I cannot possibly pay my debts and at the same time provide medical care for my family? How am I to be truthful in this situation when my boss asks me a question and my answer can harm another employee?

Evidently we need more than knowledge, the teaching of the Church, and direction of law. All these provide only general guidelines. They do not give us the concrete answers that we need in the actual unique situations of our life. These guidelines often tell us what we *cannot* do if we are to please God and follow Christ. They give us general ideas as to what we ought to do, but inevitably—and it's always been that way—it is up to us to decide what we are going to do here and now, in the situation that involves these people, these circumstances, these foreseeable consequences.

This is the critical question for every Christian. It is *the* moral question. Part of the nobility of our life is that we do have the capacity to make these judgments. We have intelligence, imagination, memory, freedom. We have a natural power, increased by experience, to act prudently. And this native power is enhanced by a gift, the virtue of prudence, which develops under the influence of the Holy Spirit. We are equipped and able to decide and act, in all the concrete situations of our life so as to respond lovingly, in Christ, to the call of the Father.

The Decision of Prudence

We can define prudence in many ways. It is a virtue that makes the other virtues *actual*. We decide to say this and not that, and we actually say what we decided. It is the virtue (habit) which moves us to make actual and real, through concrete acts, what the demands of the moment call for, in the light of Christ. For instance, I know that I should go to Mass on Sunday. (General principle.) My sick mother needs care. Is it reasonable to leave her for a while and go to Mass? How much effort and expense should I go to in getting someone to take my place? There is only one Mass available. What do I do here and now? In one case, I may prudently decide to go to Mass; in another, I may decide the prudent thing to do is to stay home with my mother.

How do I arrive at this judgment? The first thing we notice about prudence is that it always deals with a *concrete situation*, with all its uniqueness. It does not attempt to discover general principles, but *starts* with them, and attempts to realize them in specific circumstances. It *starts* with the situation and attempts to examine all the pertinent factors. What is the just thing to do to this employee at this time? He has always been faithful, but he is hindering the work of others. There is no other position open, his family needs his salary, and his retirement is far off. Yet the firm needs updating. It is losing valuable time in seeking more modern methods. All these factors, plus general principles, have to be considered.

Prudence presupposes moral knowledge, knowledge of the teachings of the Church, knowledge of Scripture, knowledge of the law. It brings the general moral law to bear on *this situation*, so that our Christian responsibility can be rightly expressed in the actual decision we make.

Response to Christ

The next thing we notice about prudence is that it deals with concrete actions precisely *in terms of our response to Christ*. My judgment

49

about meeting the demands of the moment is made precisely in terms of my desire to live my commitment to Christ. Evidently, then, Christian prudence must be enlightened by faith and powered by love of Christ. Otherwise the response will not be *to Christ*. Thus, in a particular business transaction involving a substantial profit, we may not *literally* be violating a particular law, but we may still be acting contrary to real prudence by refusing the demands of equity and taking advantage of the other person's needs. To negotiate such a deal is not prudent. It is not responding to Christ. We did not, indeed, break any one particular civil law but we sinned by violating a higher one.

Another aspect of prudence is that it is *always* operative, though we may not be conscious of it at all times. It is in more complex or confused situations that we become explicitly aware of seeking to act prudently. Thus, for instance, if someone asks us for help, and we are free and able to give it, we usually respond without much thought about prudence. In these uncomplicated situations prudence is functioning, but quickly and spontaneously, out of habit. On the other hand, if a neighbor comes for help, and I am just then ready to leave on vacation with my family, prudence will have to operate rather consciously. If I am asked to move to another city with my family or lose a promised promotion, there is no quick or spontaneous response. Now I have to consider all aspects of the matter quite deliberately.

The Opposite of Scrupulosity

I would like to reemphasize what has been said, lest scrupulous persons get the notion that the new morality would require us to make a lengthy and agonizing investigation before every judgment we make. Three things need to be said.

1) In *analyzing* a judgment of conscience, as we are doing, we are laying out all the elements on an assembly line, as it were. In reality, these elements very often go through our consciousness so fast that they seem automatic and intuitive. One of the prime requirements of prudence is that a situation be given no more attention than it is worth.

2) The reason we make these judgments so swiftly, in most cases, is that we have built up a habit—good or bad—by many previous judgments of the same kind. Any given judgment is quite a bit in line with our characteristic attitude. We don't start all over each time we face the possibility of telling a lie: we "automatically" continue our free choice of honesty. It might be said, therefore, that we "are" our attitudes. Our "good habits" (another name for virtue) is the momentum we have freely built into our lives.

3) It must also be emphasized that our judgments of conscience are not always concerned with doing arduous, challenging, painful things. If our prudence does indeed look *all* around us, we will realize the necessity of wholesome relaxation, fun, "hanging loose," "goofing off." In one situation it may be the highest response to

the will of Christ to take a nap, or have a drink, or go to the movies, as it is to attend Mass, go to confession or visit the sick in another situation. Christ asks a response from us in our total life: our leisure and our work, our prayer and our play; our artistic as well as our more earthy enjoyments.

With these three observations clearly in mind, we can try to dissect the act of prudent judgment to see what makes it tick.

Three Steps

What are the "steps" one takes, then, in being prudent? We usually list three: thinking, judging and acting.

First, *deliberation*. A prudent man will consider the matter at hand. He will ponder what *people* are involved—their needs, feelings, rights, temperament, past reactions; the *circumstances* —time, place, who is present and absent, what is going to happen soon, what has just happened; what *alternatives* there are—to act or not to act, to act in this way or that way, to do this much and no more, to act alone or with help, to act now or later; what are the various foreseeable *consequences* of these courses of actions—both the long-range and the short-range consequences. A prudent man tries to grasp the whole picture as best he can. In the background of his consideration of this situation is the general realm of his moral knowledge—his knowledge of revelation, teachings of the Church and any laws which might be involved. *Within this framework he*

looks at the whole situation.

Now, my deliberations can never be absolutely certain or perfect. I do not have unlimited time in which to deliberate. The demands of the moment do not wait. I must act. Not to act is to act. So I try to deliberate in proportion to the seriousness of the matter. I don't take all day to deliberate whether I'll light this cigarette or read this book. On the other hand, I take much more time arriving at the judgment whether or not to take on a new job, change my college major, get married or enter religious life.

Second, in time he comes to a *judgment* as to which course of action he is able to and should take to achieve his goal. He *decides* what seems to be the better way to follow Christ, here and now, and respond to God in *this* situation. He judges a particular action to be more conducive, all things considered, to producing good and avoiding evil consequences.

The *judgment* and *decision* of prudence is really identical in content with what we call the judgment of conscience. Once this decision to act in a certain way is reached, the person sees his obligation. He must carry out *this* decision. And here the moral force, the obliging character of conscience comes into play. For if I prudently judge that here and now this course of action is the better alternative, then my very vocation to follow Christ demands that I *ought* to act in that way; my conscience *obliges* me to do so or else fail in my response to Christ—and so to sin.

Thirdly, therefore, prudence requires *acting* according to the decision of conscience.

Joe Bungalow knows all the ins and outs, pros and cons, about the effects of integration on the value of neighborhood property. But he doesn't *do* anything about it! Deliberation and judging are merely means that should lead to action. On the other hand, to act precipitously, to act without sufficient deliberation and judging of alternatives would lead to imprudent or ill-considered actions.

There are many helps that we can use in order to grow in our capacity to judge and act prudently. We draw on our memory of past experiences, past judgments we have made, and their outcome. We are truly "experienced" if we actually let the lessons of the past be a factor in our present judgments.

As we grow in our Christian life, we should develop foresight and be better able to foresee obstacles and hindrances as well as undesirable consequences of our activity. As we grow older and more mature as human persons and Christians, there is a corresponding deepening of our insights into moral values, a greater openness to reality around us, and a readiness to arrive at the best decision no matter what it may demand. In all these ways we should be growing, our decisions becoming correspondingly more prudent, more responsive to Christ.

The Risk of Making Mistakes

To act prudently does not necessarily mean I

will never make a mistake, or that others will always agree with my judgment of prudence. To act prudently means that I deliberate sufficiently; I judge as best I can; I then act in the best way I know how, believing that God will accept my decision as honest and sincere. I hope I will keep growing and learning by my mistakes.

Later I may realize that my decision did not turn out well. In fact it turned out "wrong" because of a factor which I did not know about, one which I did not or could not foresee, even though I deliberated sufficiently. After prudent counsel and deliberation, using all available facts, I made the decision to appoint this person as sales manager or religious superior; I decided to buy this book, this car. I decided I was competent for this job.

Later I find that the judgment was mistaken. It was "wrong." But my effort was holy, prudent and morally good. It embodied my desire to respond to God to the best of my ability. It was all God expected.

Finally, I ought to be clearly aware that judgments of prudence often lack absolute certainty. Often there is risk involved. This should not surprise or deter us. God calls us to give our sincere response at every moment and in every situation, and in every action or omission.

At times there is no difficulty—to go to church, to give alms, to speak the truth, to love our spouse, to be patient and helpful with our children, not to kill or lie or cheat or steal. But in others it is not at all easy or clear.

Even when there are laws to guide us, or when the Church has taught something about the matter in hand, there is still difficulty in deciding what we are *actually to do concretely here and now so as to really respond to Christ*.

Let us take one example. What do I do when my wife is run down physically, when I have more children now than I can care for properly or decently, when the peace and harmony of my family is really in jeopardy for many reasons; when there is more need now than ever for my wife and I to express to each other the greatest possible love and affection? What am I to do in such a situation? How am I to act, here and now, concretely, so as to fulfill in the best way, not only this or that part of my responsibility, but *all* of my responsibilities: to my wife, to my children, to my family, to myself, to God? If I cannot fulfill all of them or if at least I cannot *see* how I possibly can, how am I to choose which one of my responsibilities is more important and so decide which course of action I am to follow. It is obvious here that something has to be done. Some decision has to be made. There is no easy solution.

Confidence

There is indeed a danger of one-sided solutions, half-hearted solutions, even selfish solutions. But I have to run this danger and risk, because there is an obligation for me to decide and to act. I must decide as best I can in the light of all I know about the teachings of revelation and the Church, about my particular situation and all my responsibilities, about my personal strength and weakness, and about the past, the present and the future. I must want to respond to Christ in whatever decisions I make. When I finally decide, I will not be absolutely sure I am not making a mistake. But I can be *morally* sure that I am doing the best I can to respond to Christ in this particular concrete situation. And any person who tries to respond in this way can be sure that he is actually pleasing to Christ.

Let us close this consideration with a thought from Fr. Bernard Häring, the eminent Redemptorist moral theologian. He stresses the fact that in the past moral theology did not emphasize enough the virtue of prudence and the gifts of the Holy Spirit in arriving at the concrete decisions in our lives. He says, "If one has failed to place any trust in the power of the Christian to recognize the loving will of God except through the universal norm of law applied to a particular case falling under the law, then it would follow that the great law of love must lose all value of obligation, except where some law explicitly applies the norm. However, the moral theology in which the teaching on the gifts of the Holy Spirit and on the virtue of prudence plays the role which it assumes in St. Thomas, such moral theology is in the best sense of the term personalistic. In such theology, a Christian does not confront a frigid impersonal law, but the divine call of grace, summoning him in this very hour. The Christian who is truly prudent, entirely docile to the inner master, the Holy Spirit, will harken to the will of God lovingly calling to him *both* in the external universal law which binds him, and in the exigency of the unique situation and in the special call of divine grace" (*Law of Christ*, I, 511).

Questions for Discussion

1. Why do we seem to identify prudence with timidity, excessive caution, standing pat?

2. Why are general principles essential and at the same time insufficient?

3. Is there, strictly speaking, such a thing as a "general" prudential decision?

4. Can you expand a bit on the "think, judge, act" principle?

5. "I am responsible for my actions, but my mistakes can come from prudential decisions." Is this possible?

6. What is the ultimate purpose of making prudent decisions?

Chapter V

Law

When the word "law" is mentioned, a great variety of ideas and fears occur to people. Some immediately think of law as particular: "Thou shalt not steal," "Speed limit—30 mph," "Must go to Mass on Sunday." The old may be concerned about the apparent disregard for law by the young; the young may feel anger at the unreasonableness and coerciveness of law.

But despite all the confusion, almost all men agree there is need for law in human society. There is much disagreement as to the nature and extent of the binding force of law, e.g. do traffic laws oblige in conscience, or in what circumstances can we judge that a law of hearing Mass does not oblige? There is further disagreement as to how we are to act when various laws seem to conflict, e.g. when the presence of fetal life endangers mother's life. Now it is precisely in confronting all these difficulties concerning laws that the "new" moral theology will emphasize very much *the* law that is above *all* other laws in our life: the law of Christ.

Christ—Our Law

"The Law of Christ" is used to mean simply that Christ—in His person and message and deeds—takes precedence over any other concern, any other law. Christ Himself is the supreme *norm* of our lives, and insofar as we have been called to follow and imitate Christ, we are *obliged* to conform all our lives and activities to Him, as norm, as "law."

It is sometimes said that "love" is the supreme norm, or "law," of our lives; or, that the "grace of the Holy Spirit" is the supreme norm, or "law," of our lives. There is no contradiction here. All three of these terms are really attempts to say the same thing. To follow Christ is to imitate someone whose whole life was an expression of love. So, to make "love" the supreme norm of my life is to live by "the Law of Christ." Similarly, since the whole intent of the Holy Spirit in showering His graces upon us is to lead us to an ever more complete following of Christ, we can see that responding to the grace of the Holy Spirit is to fulfill "the Law of Christ."

So, the first thing a Christian must understand in any discussion of law is that the *primary law of our life is Christ*. This is the basic fact of Christian morality. To respond to Him is the overriding consideration of our whole existence. To live in His love, to respond to Him, is absolutely our prime concern. Everything else is secondary. We are to live as He lived, love as He loved.

St. Paul reflects Christ's teaching. "Keep out of debt altogether except that perpetual debt of love which we owe one another. The man who loves his neighbor has obeyed the whole law in regard to his neighbor. For the commandments, thou shalt not commit adultery, thou shalt not kill, thou shalt not steal, thou shalt not covet, *and all other commandments* are summed up in this one saying, 'Thou shalt love thy neighbor as thyself.' Love hurts nobody. Therefore love is the answer to the law's demands." It is only in the light of Christ, our First Law, that we can understand and appreciate what *other* laws are all about. Many people express fear in a discussion of law today. Some think we are trying to throw out all laws. But what we are really attempting is to see them in their proper perspective, to better appreciate their true role. We want to see laws as norms and supports in the one most important thing of our lives, following Christ. They are to serve that purpose, not take precedence over it. It is a question of a very basic orientation to laws.

There is admittedly much confusion about laws today. But in *any* discussion or consideration of the nature, function, binding force of any law, the words of Christ and Paul just quoted must be given their full weight, and never forgotten. Otherwise we are quite likely to end up with some kind of legalism, some kind of

morality that—whatever else it may be—does not truly or fully reflect the Gospel, and so cannot be fully Christian.

Much of the confusion about laws and the observance of laws is due to quite drastically different starting points, as was pointed out in the first chapter. Those who follow the new morality give absolute primacy to love, person, community. They seek to achieve and promote these primary values in the concrete. This they understand as the law of Christ; this above all they understand as acting responsibly. All other laws and norms—whatever they may be—are understood as subordinate and secondary, and accepted as valid only insofar as they protect or promote primary values.

Part of the confusion about laws is also due to the fact that there are different kinds of laws. There are divine positive laws, natural laws, Church laws, civil laws. There are affirmative laws, negative laws, invalidating laws, etc. No wonder we tend to be confused, even if we have a healthy attitude toward laws. We tend to become preoccupied with these laws, and forget all too much *the* most important law of all.

Then, too, there are so *many* laws, some outdated and meaningless; others so detailed and minute as to be almost impossible to observe. It is a very hopeful sign that Church law is now being drastically renewed.

Natural Law

But the confusion becomes all the greater

68

when there is discussion of the "natural law." Outside of the Catholic Church, there is little, if any, real acceptance of the whole idea of natural law. Even within the Catholic Church there have always been different understandings of the natural law at different times. In the light of the vastly different starting points mentioned in the first chapter, the differences are becoming significantly greater today. If the discussants do not recognize this, little progress can be made.

It is important to realize that the Church arrived at many of her moral doctrines without natural law theory. It was only after the Middle Ages, and most especially after the 16th century, that moral theologians began more and more to use a natural law theory to "explain" the moral teachings of the Church. It is only in the last century that Popes began to put great stress on moral teaching and moral norms as being formulations of the natural law.

This natural law theory assumes that the very will of God for man is somehow "written" into his very nature, so that man, through the use of his reason, is able to discern what human nature means. Thus he can know how to act—according to nature—and so fulfill the natural law. Part of the difficulty with such a theory is that it presupposed that reason *could* deduce the norms for good human actions from an abstract understanding of human nature. At the same time it stressed the moral necessity of revelation for us to know these norms with certainty and without error.

69

Further difficulties arose from the readiness of theologians to identify some norm as "of the natural law," and from the fact that natural law theory gave very little consideration to the unique and concrete aspects of human situations. But most of all, the difficulty with the natural law theory is that it has been developed with a very particular understanding of "human nature," an understanding which is radically different from the modern view of man as personal, free, becoming, historical, contingent.

The Problem of Absoluteness

By far the most difficult aspect of natural law theory is the "universal, negative norms" of natural law. These are the principles that forbid some determined action, and are held to bind *all* men at *all* times and in *all* circumstances. Such norms *never* admit of any possible exception; they bind absolutely. Such, for example, are the norms forbidding the direct killing of the innocent, direct sterilization, lying, adultery, fornication, masturbation, homosexuality.

Perhaps you will say at once: "Why all those are immoral!" Agreed. But I refer to them as the most difficult aspect of natural law theory—not in that they are binding norms—but in that they are declared to be *absolutely* binding, and never under any circumstances admit of exception. It is this point that disturbs proponents of the new morality. They stress certain norms, too, but stress even more the *values* underlying these norms. But it is in terms of love and person and community that they stress these values, and so cannot quite conceive how they can be *absolute*.

Thus, for example, it can happen that a mother of six living young children is pregnant, and circumstances are such that it is humanly impossible to save *both* the life of the mother *and* the fetus. The proponents of the new morality cannot see how it is really the more loving thing to let the mother die, with all the consequences of this deliberate omission, rather than directly remove the child. This kind of exceptional situation can be multiplied in other areas.

In all this discussion I have obviously not settled anything—and perhaps have only added to the confusion—but I do hope I have helped the reader see some of the difficulties involved, and especially *why* those who follow the new morality have such grave difficulty not only with the absoluteness of the norms, but also with the natural law theory itself.

The new morality, as indicated, is much more concerned with values, such as life, marital fidelity and love, honesty, justice, peace. It is concerned about law only insofar as laws really protect and promote these values. The whole question of laws would make more sense if this perspective were maintained. But there is another consideration here. That is the *changing* hierarchy of values in the world today, and especially among those who hold the new morality. Thus, for example, the value of life has always been stressed by the Church. But many

feel today that, while the value of life yet un-
born is to be guarded, there is great incon-
sistency when fetal life is so stressed that other
forms of killing receive too little attention, e.g.
war, capital punishment. If fetal life is an absolute value, then why not life already born?

Or again, there has been in the past an extra-
ordinary preoccupation with understanding the
whole realm of sexuality in terms of procreation, and this in terms of the "correctness" of
the act of intercourse according to its physical
and biological structure. Yet today, when popu-
lation has become such a problem, such a stress
seems inconsistent. Along this same line, when
psychology and sociology have amassed such
overwhelming evidence of the criticalness of the
love relationship between husband and wife in
providing children with the kind of atmosphere
of love necessary for normal growth and development, it seems that the loving relation of
parents is a higher value than procreation.

The Ten Commandments

The confusion and difficulty I have tried to
indicate concerning the absolute norms of the
natural law, and the natural law theory itself, are
directly related to divine positive law, as proclaimed in the Ten Commandments. For almost
all the norms deduced from natural law theory
are said to be identical with the content of the
Ten Commandments. (The Ten Commandments
are called divine positive laws because they are
explicitly promulgated by God through the

sacred writer.) Perhaps it would be helpful at this point to stress again the orientation of the new morality toward Christ as *the* Law, and toward the values found in the Ten Commandments as seen in the light of Christ.

The new morality stresses that Christ came to proclaim the will of God in its full and absolute sense: namely, that no law can take precedence over His will, His kingdom. Jesus stressed this fact. He said to the Scribes and Pharisees, "You've made a sort of laughing stock out of the law. You've made the law and your traditions more important than the will of God. That's turning things upside down."

Christ stressed interiority, the observance of the law coming from the heart. "You can observe the law wholeheartedly only when you are seeking to do the will of God your Father." It is what comes out of the heart of a man that can defile him. He stressed that love of God and neighbor is the fulfillment of all law, and that all other laws are subordinate to love of God and men. St. Paul stressed the very same ideas—the fact that mere observance of the laws cannot save us. Salvation comes only from the mercy and grace of God, through our faith and responsiveness.

In this sense, then, the divine positive law, the laws given by God in the Old Testament, ceased with the inauguration of the New Covenant in Christ. Yet the important values those laws entailed—especially in the Ten Commandments—are just as valid as ever. These values are bound up with our very nature as human persons. No one follows Christ and really loves his neighbor if he disregards these values, i.e., giving glory to God and His Holy Name, respecting human life, living honestly and justly, etc. The values of the Ten Commandments are still to be pursued by those following Christ, but pursued in the light of Christ Himself.

The Underlying Values

Thus, for example, the Fifth Commandment, in the Old Covenant reads: "Thou shalt not kill." The value here is reverence for life—human life. How do we understand this in the New Covenant? We look at Jesus' life and see that He came not to be served but to serve and to *give His own life* as a ransom for many (so much did He value human life). We are caught up in this life of Christ; we too want to give our life in the service of God and our brethren. So the first thing we Christians ought to do, in accordance with the Fifth Commandment, is to *give away our lives in the service of God and neighbor*, to spend them. Because I want to do this in the fullest and most fruitful way, I will take care of my life. I will try not to be careless lest I injure my life and thus hinder or destroy my ability to serve God and my neighbor.

Thus Christ, being the center and law of our life, gives a whole new cast to the value involved in the Fifth Commandment.

Or, take the Eighth Commandment. We say it means we must not lie. But what does this mean in the New Covenant?

We have been made in God's image and likeness, given a share in God's life. That means to share in the truth. But only to the extent that we are alive in Christ who is the Truth, will we be in the truth. Only to the extent that we are trying to live as Christians will we be living *truth*fully. We begin in this way to appreciate our gift of speech, in which we use our whole selves—lips, tongue, throat, intelligence and memory—whenever we utter a word. If we want to be like Christ, we will utter a truthful word. And if we will mirror the life of the Trinity in our own life, we will utter a truthful word *lovingly*. We'll never speak the truth without love, and we will never love except truthfully. In this sense, then, we begin to see the terrible malice of lying, of deception and of all untruthfulness.

Again let us emphasize: *Christ* is the law of our life, and the moral values found in revelation have to be understood in terms of following Christ. It is He who makes the difference in our understanding and our observance of all laws.

Human Law

We turn now to human law—church or civil law. Again, this kind of law, and our obedience, makes sense only in terms of following Christ. Obeying human law must be an expression of our response to Christ.

We can say without question that human laws are necessary because of our social nature, the communitarian aspect of our personal existence. Perhaps, too, because of our weakness and sinfulness we need the support of law. Thus, for example, we have civil laws regulating contracts, property ownership, use of drugs.

The one thing that must be stressed here is that human laws, whether they are laws of the Church or of civil society, are *human*. They are not perfect. They cannot be perfect. They are not absolute, and they cannot be absolute. They are not the most important consideration of our lives; they cannot be.

So, we have to test human laws, to decide whether or not the observance of them is in harmony with our basic and overriding concern to follow Christ.

This is not to say that we do not respect human law, or that we do not have an attitude of loving obedience to the laws of Church and civil society. Indeed, the Christian should be quite aware that all authority is from God, and so obedience to all just laws is an expression of loving obedience to God. At the same time we are mindful that human laws are imperfect instruments. They are made by human beings and bound up with concrete historical circumstances. For example, the laws regulating child labor can be understood only in terms of the historical situation that prevailed at the time they were made.

Again, Problems

Even though human laws are imperfect and

subject to change, they can promote the general good. They are guidelines to help us avoid harming others and to show us ways of giving ourselves to others. Human laws are ways in which we can express our obedience to our heavenly Father: paying taxes, obeying traffic laws, heeding the laws of society on drugs, narcotics and firearms, observing the laws of the Church with regard to Mass on Sunday, confession, and so on.

These are helps for us to do good. They remind us of our basic responsibility as human beings and Christians. *But* they are not designed merely for conformity or uniformity. They cannot remove personal responsibility. For example, my responsibility to my parents or children may oblige me *not* to go to Mass on a given Sunday.

Human laws cannot truly be obeyed if we do not know something about why they exist, their ends and purposes. For example, just to go to church and be present at Mass is not enough; the very purpose of this law is to get us to worship God. If we do not actively participate in worshiping God, we cannot say we have obeyed the law.

We should be aware that human laws can at times allow actions that are evil; in that case we could not morally do what the law allows. Our present abortion laws would be among such laws. This is the law in some states; yet it would be morally wrong to have an abortion, even when state law permits it.

Human laws can become outdated. The Church has seen very definite need for updating her law, to bring it into conformity with modern circumstances. For instance, a Mass was formerly not permitted for the wedding of a Catholic and a non-Catholic. Now this may be done. Again, according to Canon 607, Sisters were not to be allowed to leave the house alone, except in case of necessity. This surely needed to be updated.

Human laws can come into conflict with higher laws. As a priest I am obliged to say the Divine Office every day. But if on a given day I would refuse to take a dying person to the hospital because I had to recite my breviary, I would obviously be doing wrong. I would not really be pleasing God by saying those prayers even though I obeyed that one particular law. The farmer whose crop is ready for harvesting knows that a day's delay may mean the loss of his whole crop. The law says he shouldn't work on Sunday. But a greater law says he should take care of his family. So that farmer might be doing wrong by not working on Sunday.

Again, human laws cannot possibly take into consideration all the particular and concrete situations of people, time and place. Human laws legislate for general conditions. I must reckon with this when it comes to observing human laws. The law says I must fast from food an hour before Communion. But if it's my wedding day and I forget about fasting and eat something, I certainly should go to Communion

80

under those circumstances. The lawmaker was not envisioning those particular concrete circumstances of mine. He expected me to use my intelligence in such a situation.

In these and many other ways, we see that the Christian has a respect for law, but at the same time is vitally aware that the supreme law of life is Christ. The supreme law is to love God and his neighbor. Every other law is subordinate to that. All human laws must be understood in terms of Christ, in terms of people, and of what is best for people. We must make a practical judgment in each case. Oftentimes, of course, there is no real problem. It's often a very simple thing. There's the law: I do what it says, I don't do what it forbids.

Sometimes I am selfish or weak, and consciously I disobey the law. But in that case I know that I am guilty. In many other situations it's not so easy. Sometimes I don't know what this law means, what it is trying to achieve. Thus, perhaps I do not grasp very well what the law of Sunday Mass is meant to achieve; I do not really understand how my life as a Christian is rooted in and expressed in the Eucharist. Consequently, the law of Sunday Mass doesn't make too much sense to me. Or again, maybe I know what this law means and is trying to achieve, but I don't see how I can achieve that purpose in the situation in which I find myself. For example, I know and understand the purpose of inheritance tax laws. But if I follow these laws literally with regard to my grandfather's estate, some members of the family will be deprived of money they seriously need. So I have to make some adjustment. This is the judgment of prudence which we spoke of. What *would* be the better thing for me to do? To follow the letter of the law, or to depart from the letter of the law believing that by so doing I can really do what is best.

Guidelines

The following may serve as guidelines when I run into these difficult situations. When I don't see how the law applies here, when I don't see how I can observe the letter of the law in this case and still do the better thing, I should ask myself: 1) What is my reason for not observing the letter of the law? Am I just being selfish, or do I have a sufficient reason? For example, the law forbids a priest to hear the confession of a woman outside the confessional. But there can be a real necessity for doing so, e.g. this woman is terribly afraid of going into the dark cubicle. 2) Will I achieve some equal or greater good by not observing the letter of the law? Will my action, which does not fulfill the letter of the law, really be more in keeping with the purpose of the law and my following of Christ? For example, a priest is forbidden to distribute Communion under both species apart from specified occasions. But on the occasion of a home Mass for a very special family celebration, I may decide it would be *better* to distribute under both species precisely because I mean to emphasize the value and meaning of the sacramental sign.

Our basic attitude, then, in terms of the new emphasis in moral theology is: I want to be Christian. I want to follow Christ. I want my life, as far as possible, to be one of love for God and for neighbor. I recognize and accept the fact that there's a place for law in my life—the law of my human nature, the natural law, God's positive law, the laws of civil society and the Church. Basically I want to observe these, whenever I can, to the best of my ability. I need the guidance of law.

But I am also aware that I have to judge all laws in terms of Christ. Merely to do what the letter of the law says is no guarantee that I am following Christ in a particular instance. Merely to follow the letter of the law does not necessarily mean that I am fulfilling the spirit and purpose of the law. Merely to blindly observe the letter of the law does not free me from my personal responsibility.

I respect laws, I am grateful for the guidance of laws. Laws can give me much help and support, but in the end, I am going to have to answer as to how I responded to Christ. That's the overriding question. All laws are subordinate to that. All laws must be judged in this light, and judged by each one of us as best we can.

Command and/or Counsel

From this brief consideration of law, one thing ought to be clear. The "new morality"

views the *whole* of one's life as involved in response to God's call. My Christian vocation is to live the whole of my life as response to God. Accordingly, the ever-present question in the Christian's heart is: What does God want or expect of me here and now? What is the call in this present moment of grace? How do I best promote the values of love, community, peace—in terms of who I am, the people involved and all the circumstances.

Thus, Mike is talking with a friend. The command not to lie or deceive or slander obviously is an instance of God's will for him here and now. But the positive command to speak the truth forces Mike to make some further decisions as to what would please God; what truths should he utter, to what extent; what truth would violate confidence, etc. To do God's will—Mike's vocation—it is not enough for Mike not to lie.

Another example: Mary has prayed, searched her heart, consulted with others for a long time, and now she is morally sure that she should become a nun. In concrete cases such as this, the new emphasis in morality would maintain that there is an obligation to respond. There is certainty of judgment here (granting the distinction between command and counsel when speaking of the Christian life *in general*) that God is asking for something from her.

God is not indifferent to the way in which I respond to Him. This present moment does involve some kind of call from God, a call to say

Yes to Him in some concrete way. *I am not free to ignore this call*, even if it is only a matter of chatting with a neighbor, or giving the baby his bottle. I cannot label as "only an imperfection" my conscious and deliberate neglect of actions that I recognize I am capable of doing, and which I judge that my situation calls for. What does it mean to live according to the Spirit if my only source of obligation is external law? Why do we speak of faithfulness to the inspirations of grace and docility to the Holy Spirit?

In the older approach to morality, we seemed to say: Do what the Commandments tell you to do, avoid what they tell you to avoid, keep all the laws, and that's pretty much all that is really required. In the rest of your life you are on your own. In contrast, we begin to appreciate the orientation and emphasis of the "new morality." It is not an "easy" morality. Keeping the Commandments, the laws, especially the negative ones, is a bare minimum, never enough. God calls for our whole heart, our whole life, at every moment. The Christian is one who seeks to respond always to this call, even when no "laws" are evident. Every moment, in all he does, the Christian creates his response to God.

What I actually do may not be a "big deal" at all. It may be something very ordinary: going to the drug store, serving on the parish council, attending a party, etc. But whatever it is, whatever I judge to be the "right" thing to do in any particular situation, I choose to do it.

Questions *for Discussion*

1. How does the "Law that is Christ" oblige us?

2. Is the principle "Christ is our Law" sufficient to enable us to make all judgments of conscience?

3. How do we arrive at an awareness of what natural law is? What is the greatest problem about its obligatory force?

4. What do you mean by a "value"? How are values acquired? How are they taught?

5. What values are safeguarded by the individual Ten Commandments?

6. Can I find myself obliged to do something not actually required by a particular law?

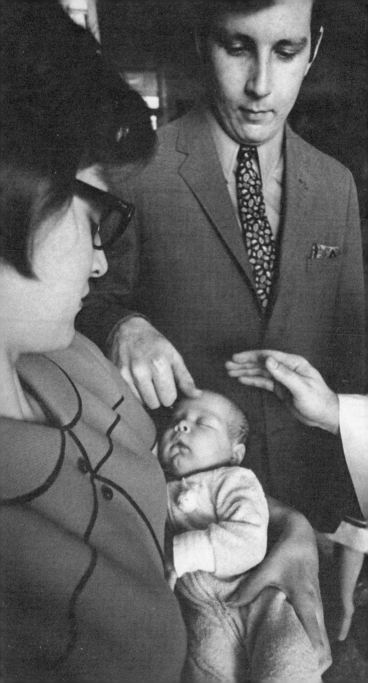

Chapter VI

Love

In the New

Morality

there are many laws and regulations in Church, state and family that guide our lives. The pastor, for instance, has regulations from his bishop; the taxpayer from his government; the teenager from his parents. But with all these regulations, as we have seen, the Christian must ever be mindful that there is one law above all other laws, one to which all other laws take second place: *the law of Christ*, or to put it another way, the law of love.

In treating law in the last chapter, we indicated something of the relationship between law and love in the New Covenant. Now we want to focus on the sources of Christian love and some of the characteristics it should have.

There is so much said about love today that we get tired of it all. Sometimes we are given the impression that love was discovered for the first time in 1960. At other times we are disturbed that some of the people who talk the most about love seem to practice it the least. Despite all this, we know that loving God and people is what our life is all about. There is no such thing as giving the real virtue too much attention.

Where It Originates

First, then, we consider the *source* of Christian love—the fact that *God* is love. Sometimes the most simple and obvious facts tend to escape us. We hear, go away and forget what we heard. *God is love*. We think, "That's true! That's great!" and promptly forget it.

What could be more important? God is love. God's whole life is loving. God is Father and Son and Spirit. These three distinct persons exist in perfect love and communion; they give themselves to each other, receive from each other, and share life so perfectly that the Bible can say simply: God is love.

But it can escape us that we are called to share in the life of this God. That is the very nature of our Christian vocation. We are called to live like God. We are called to a life of love. Everything else in our lives makes sense only in terms of this, that we are called to live and grow in love, to bring forth fruit in love for the life of the world. God did not create us merely to go through certain motions, to fulfill obligations only, to be good robots. To achieve great wisdom, earn great wealth, exercise great power is not enough. In fact, without love, it is nothing. To care for the young, to minister to the sick, to come to the aid of the poor and needy, in short, to love our neighbor: *this* is why we exist. This is what our life in Christ is all about.

God's love is revealed in Jesus Christ. God not only told us that He is love; He also loved the world so much that He sent His Son, and the Word was made flesh and dwelt among us. Jesus is the revelation of the Father's love, the incarnation (actually the "en-flesh-ment") of the Father's love.

We can set the scene for a discussion of the qualities of Christian love by recalling the words of St. John: "We know and to some extent realize the love of God for us, because Christ expressed it in laying down his life for us. We must in turn express our love by laying down our lives for those who are our brothers. Let us love not merely in theory or in words, let us love in sincerity and in practice" (I John 3:14 ff.).

"To you whom I love," St. John says, "let us go on loving one another because love comes from God" (I John 4:7).

God, the Source of All Love

This is the first and most important characteristic of Christian love: *it comes from God*.

God loves us *first*, and in His loving us we are brought to life. We are given the capacity to love in response. "The love of God has been poured into our hearts by the Holy Spirit who has been given to us" (Romans 5:5). We have received the command to love one another as Jesus loves us. God accepts our love for our neighbor as love expressed to Jesus. "What you

91

do to the least of these, my brethren, you do unto me." Loving is not something "extra" added to our life in Christ. Human love for human persons is the very expression of our life in Christ. That is why Jesus could say, through St. John, "If you don't love your brothers, whom you see, who are right next to you, how can you say you love God, whom you don't see?" (Cf. I John 4:20). "Let us love one another, because love is from God" (I John 4:7).

We can go a step further: as in Jesus the Father's love was made incarnate and embodied, so to speak, in human form, so too our love is to be a kind of "incarnation" of God's love for us, making it visible, giving it flesh. When we love another person, and realize that our love has its source in God, we are making incarnate—"giving flesh to"—God's love for that person. When I love another human being in the real sense, as Christ loves me, I am in a way continuing the incarnation of Christ for that person.

Our Love Is Human

This makes us stress that our love must be *human* love. It must be Godlike—as we say, divine—but it must also be human. Sometimes we have so stressed the divine aspect that we neglect the human. If our neighbor is hungry, we give him something to eat; we satisfy his *human* appetite, not directly a supernatural one. In the past, we often failed to give *human* affection to our human neighbors. Instead, we gave them a rather formal, "charitable" treatment that some-how fulfilled our "obligation."

We have sometimes made much of the dis-tinction between "loving" and "liking." "I love him, but I don't have to like him"—as if we could love a man's soul and "hate his guts." His soul supposedly existed in frozen purity some-where apart from his body, his feelings, his language and his opinions. To love as Christ loves is to love both divinely and humanly. I can be overflowing with "supernatural" motivation and still fail when it comes right down to giving my neighbor what Christ wants me to give him—genuine human affection.

Often it is not so much our prayers that a neighbor wants at a given moment—still less our "supernatural good intention." He wants a little understanding or affection. Under the guise of "Well, I'll pray for you," we can shrink from the effort required for sincere love. If a man is hungry, it is not love just to pray for him, or to say that his soul is more important than his body. If a man needs our love, companionship, help, it will not be proper for us to substitute a Holy Hour for actually taking care of his needs.

It is hardly compassion to see someone being beaten on the street and pass by without doing anything. It is hardly love to amass millions and be uncaring about the poor in the world. It is hardly love merely to pass out food stamps to those living in degrading circumstances. It is hardly love to live comfortably in the suburbs and ignore the ghetto. Loving is hard work; it

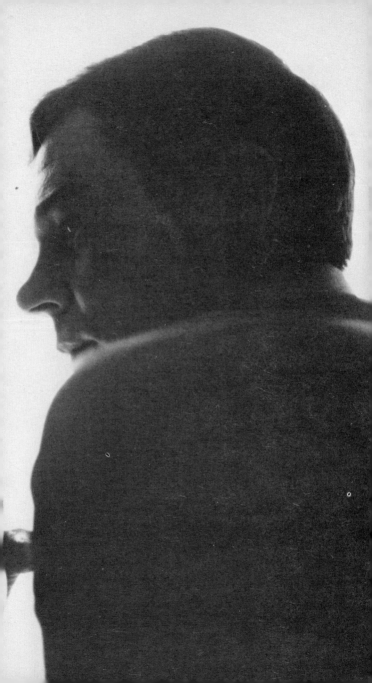

can make very unsettling and very discomforting demands on us, as it did on Jesus.

We can go a step further: our love must also be a *redemptive* love. If we are to love one another as Jesus loves us, then we are necessarily bound up in the whole process of redemption. He redeemed us through a love that led Him to give Himself up for us in suffering and death. We are to love one another with that kind of love. Our loving of the brethren is actually a way in which we share in the redeeming work of Christ. We have experienced moments of sorrow and discouragement. At such times a genuine expression of love from another person does heal us and give us new life. What we have received, that we are to give.

Loving Needs Knowing

Thirdly, love presupposes *knowledge*. You cannot review a book if you haven't read it. You cannot go out to a human person unless, to some real extent, you know that person. Often it's because we don't know much about others that we find such great difficulty in loving them; or we know only what is exterior, and superficial: the way they talk, the way they fix their hair, the kind of clothes they wear. But we haven't discovered their deep-down goodness. We don't really know them, so we find difficulty in loving them. Love presupposes that we seek to know the person we love. The very effort to know that person more deeply is a work of love.

Of course, in seeking to know other persons,

we do not invade them. We don't demand that they sit down and reveal their innermost thoughts so we can love them. Love is a gentle, gradual process. But it is important for us to realize that knowledge is a characteristic of love, and an important one. Often the difficulties between a husband and wife, or parent and child, arise simply because they do not know each other. There is no real understanding. They don't really know what's going on inside the other person, what his thoughts, feelings, attitudes are. So they find great difficulty in loving one another.

Love Respects

Fourthly—and this is a very important characteristic of love—love requires respect. The more we come to know another person and are able to go out in love to him, the more we need to respect him. Respect is a kind of warm reverence. Respect is that quality of love which never lets us *use* another person or treat him as if he were a thing. For example, the young man who in any way tries to take advantage of his date is *using* her. He does not respect her as he should. Respect is reverence for the dignity of the person before us. When our love has this quality of respect and reverence for the other person, it will be human, warm and wholesome.

Love Accepts

This leads us to a fifth characteristic of love: *acceptance* which is very much bound up with

knowledge and respect. If we are really to love one another as Jesus loves us, we must accept one another.

Very often we don't actually accept one another. We don't welcome the other person as he or she really is. Often we get twisted up by what we think the other person *ought* to be. Then we find it hard to love him. And yet the one thing that we are called to do, in imitation of Christ, is to love others *as they are*. In fact, this is the only way, realistically, that we can love them. If I am only loving what I think the other person ought to be, then I am loving something in my imagination, not the real person here before me. I'm loving my image of that person.

To love others as Christ loves us is to accept them as they are. Here we have the perennial human difficulty of accepting a person who is a "sinner." For example, parents may fail in this regard in their attitude toward a son who is married outside the Church.

How can I love such a one? We tend to turn away, shut them out. Yet we are called to love each as he or she really is. If they are sinful (and that is not our judgment to make) then we love sinful persons.

This need not in any way indicate approval for what is wrong. That is usually quite clear. But we must love the person who may have done wrong. What we sometimes forget in such cases is that we do not actually know for sure that another person is *guilty* of sin, even though their outward actions are wrong. But even on the supposition that they are certainly guilty, our attitude must be one of love and acceptance; we must love sinful persons, not because they are sinners but because they are persons.

In this connection, we sometimes find a strange overgrowth in our love for others. It's the idea that we love people "for God's sake," or that we "love Christ" in our neighbor. These expressions are not really false, but they can give a false impression. They may seem to say: "I don't really love this person before me. (He isn't worth loving, really?) I somehow look over his shoulder and love Christ whom I imagine to be standing behind." "I don't really love this person for himself, but I imagine some empty space inside him where the Father and Son and Holy Spirit dwell. I love the Trinity in him." And we never get around to really loving *this human person for himself*. Yet Jesus said "Love your neighbor. Love this body-soul person right in front of you. Love your wife, your husband, this father, this mother, this neighbor." Certainly that means "Love them as they are and love them for themselves."

In other words, my loving others is *not a means* to my own holiness. Loving others *is* my holiness. Jesus didn't intend others to be stepping stones to our holiness, "material" out of which I can manufacture holiness. We don't love others just in order to become holy ourselves or to "gain merit." That would not be Christlike. I love John because of who he is; I love him for himself. It is the *activity* of loving that is Godlike, holy.

Love Is Mercy

Another quality of love is *mercy*. If there is one thing that is clear to us, it is that we desperately need God's love, because we ourselves are sinners. The amazing fact is that God first loves us—"It was while we were sinners that Christ died for us" (Romans 5:8). It is hard for us to get this into our bones—that a very special aspect of God's love for us is that it is a merciful and forgiving love, and that Jesus really meant what He said, "Love one another now, as I have loved you." Without question, then, our love for one another must be a love full of mercy. We have received mercy, therefore we should give it.

Time after time we approach God in the sacrament of confession. Again and again we get on our knees, admit that we are sinners and beg for mercy. We rejoice in receiving God's mercy and forgiveness over and over again. And yet we sometimes forget that to receive God's mercy is to become responsible for giving that mercy to others. "You are to be merciful as your heavenly Father is merciful," Jesus tells us.

Here again, so many things can confuse us. If we've been hurt—really or only in imagination—we find it very difficult to forgive. If someone says something about us that is not true, if we are misunderstood or misjudged, we become quite incensed and upset, and it is very difficult for us to accept what happened and to love

101

those who misjudge us, with a merciful and forgiving love. We find it very hard to be like Jesus, who could say to those who nailed Him to a cross, "Father, forgive them, for they know not what they do." We are reluctant to take seriously Jesus' words to the Pharisees: "Go and learn what this means: I desire mercy and not sacrifice."

One thing that causes difficulty is a distorted sense of justice. So-and-so—my wife, my husband, my child, parent, neighbor—did something wrong. He committed a sin. How can I forgive him? How can I be merciful? How can I act as if this didn't happen?

Sometimes we almost act as if we are sent by God to wreak vengeance on others, to teach them a lesson, put them in their place, make sure they realize the wrong they've done. Because of this distorted sense of justice, we fail to be merciful, and to love them as Jesus loved us. St. Paul says, "Be kind to one another, and merciful, generously forgiving one another as God in Christ has generously forgiven you" (Eph. 4:32).

To love others mercifully is to love them with patience, to support them in their weakness, and to heal them in their woundedness. Between husband and wife, there are many instances of misunderstandings arising from failure to communicate, of hurt feelings because of thoughtlessness. They know each other so well they also get to know the weaknesses, peculiarities, failures, even the sinfulness of the partner very well. Each forgets that the others' needs are like his own: the need for patience, healing, support. If we are to love one another as Jesus loves us, then our love must certainly be a merciful love.

Love Is Kind

Another quality of Christlike love is that it be kind. St. Matthew tells us that Jesus came not so much to be served, as to serve, and to give His life as a ransom for many. Love means service.

This is the positive side of Christian love. Sometimes we think that if we don't hurt other people, if we don't misjudge them, or cause embarrassment or discomfort, don't destroy their good name, etc., that we are practicing love—and that's all there is to it. But this is only the negative side, only the barest minimum. Obviously, love demands that we do not hurt others, but it positively demands a whole lot more. Love must express itself by positive service. Love must lead us to *do* good to others, all others, even our enemies. Then only do we really show we care about people. Kindness, it seems, is best expressed through thoughtfulness and helpfulness.

To be kind is to be mindful of others. We must first open our eyes and hearts to other people, just as they are, and be sensitive to their feelings, their joys and troubles, their needs. Then we can go out to them. For example: kindness means answering letters, stopping in to see a sick person, returning borrowed articles, noticing the wife's new dress, sensing a coworker's discouragement. To love kindly requires no wealth, no education. It simply requires that we have enough self-forgetfulness so that we can open our eyes and hearts to others.

Thoughtfulness, of course, must overflow into practical expressions of love. As John says, "We must love not just in theory and words, but in practice (I John 3:18). And so thoughtfulness must be complemented by helpfulness. Just to be aware of my neighbor's need is not enough; I should give him positive help. For example, I can lend him my car when his car is in the garage. I can be very thoughtful, but if I never act out my thoughtfulness, my love is rather sterile.

On the other hand, it is possible to be helpful without being thoughtful. Then I step on people's toes and my "loving" efforts can be quite discomforting and embarrassing to others. I "inflict" my kindness on others. For instance, if someone is sick, I can annoy him by excessive visiting.

Love Is Creative

Christian love is *creative*. We sometimes forget what happens in the heart of a human person when that person receives real love. A whole new life begins. All kinds of doors and windows are opened; dark corners are illumined with new light. There is hope after all. When I have failed, made a mess of things, and then receive genuine love from someone, I gain the courage to pick up the pieces and begin again. The wife whose whole world collapses when her husband dies, can come to life again through the love of another man. Children whose parents are dead may suffer much if they do not receive real love from foster parents.

What shows more clearly than anything else that our love is from God is its being creative. If it brings new life and hope, and moves another person to grow and develop according to his talents and capacities, then it is continuing God's creation.

St. Paul says, "Love hopes all things, love never gives up" (I Cor. 13:7). That is the creative aspect of our love. When a parent, for instance, loves a teenage daughter or son, *really* loves him, really communicates the fact that he believes in this person, the parent is creating life. No matter what failures occur, no matter how many times he is let down, he never stops loving. This is creative love that gives new life; this is Christlike love.

Love Is Humble

A final characteristic of Christian love is that it is humble. Sometimes we wonder why, when we "go out and love" another person—for instance, the brother I have lived with for many years, and I have tried very hard to love—the love never quite comes off. I never come through to him. He always seems to resist my efforts.

Maybe I ought to investigate the *way* I am loving him. Perhaps I am somewhat proud, self-

sufficient, condescending. Maybe I don't really give him the impression that his acceptance of my love is his gift *to me*, for which I am humbly grateful. Maybe it doesn't come through to him, that the privilege is mine, and that I hope he will allow me to give him my love. I must not be demanding, or aloof, or proud, or puffed up.

Christian love ought to be a love that is willing to suffer. When we look at Jesus in the Gospels, we are struck by the fact that throughout His life, in His love for us, He suffered. So also, if we are to love others as Jesus loved us, we have to have the same experience. The pain comes in many ways. The husband finds his wife not fully understanding how he *feels*; the wife experiences the pain of her husband apparently not being interested in the way she *feels*, and in what goes on in her day. It should not surprise us that, as we try to love others as Jesus loved us, we will experience suffering. Maybe this is very intimately connected with the redemptive aspect of our love. It may also be much involved in the purification of our love. Maybe it is a challenge to us to grow in love; maybe it is a sign that our love is still far from perfect.

Perhaps here we have the heart of Christian asceticism: to love another person, to give of ourselves, requires that we be self-less. To say Yes to another person often means saying No to oneself. To love demands self-control. We cannot give ourselves except insofar as we possess ourselves. This coming into the possession of oneself, so as to be able to love more fully, is a painful process requiring self-discipline. This is another aspect of the pain and suffering involved in loving.

In the new morality, then, love is stressed as the absolutely primary value in our lives. Loving, loving human persons, loving others in a way that builds community is what our life is all about. To act responsibly is to act out of loving concern for real people, convinced that this is the task given us by God. It is in loving that we find Christ.

Loving does not go on "up there" somewhere, or in a vacuum, but in the flesh-and-blood world we live in, the concrete circumstances of our life. You and I are called here and now, at every moment, to live our whole life in love.

In whatever the circumstances we find ourselves: a parent with a very difficult teenager; a teenager with a very difficult parent; whether you are a man who loves a woman or a woman who loves a man; whatever your situation, you have to love that other person. That's the Good News!

This is a task that demands that we "die," many and many a time. It is also a call that leads to new life.

My dear people,
let us love one another
since love comes from God
and everyone who loves is begotten by God
and knows God.

Anyone who fails to love can never have
known God,
because God is love.
God's love for us was revealed
when God sent into the world his only Son
so that we could have life through him;
this is the love I mean:
not our love for God,
but God's love for us when he sent his Son
to be the sacrifice that takes our sins away.
My dear people,
since God has loved us so much,
we too should love one another.

(I John 4, 7-11)

Questions for Discussion

1. Can human love be like God's love?

2. Is it enough to "love" people, or must one
   "like" them?

3. At judgment, will Christ tell us He is reward-
   ing us for seeing Him in others?

4. What does it mean, actually, to forgive someone?

5. What instances of the "love that creates"
   have you seen or experienced?

6. Why is suffering involved in our desire to love
   each other?

Conclusion

In the foregoing chapters I have made no attempt to give a complete picture of Christian morality nor to deal with particular moral problems. Rather, I have tried to focus on the positive and basic foundations of Christian morality.

My conviction is this: unless we have some grasp of these positive and basic foundations, we will not be able to understand why moral theology is changing. We will not be able to struggle adequately with particular moral problems, e.g. civil disobedience, conscientious objection to war, contraception. We will not understand the approaches being taken in some schools.

St. Paul says, "Walk in a manner worthy of your calling." Christian morality has always taken this seriously, but there is much more emphasis today on our Christian vocation. We see Christ as the center of our lives; we view every moral question in terms of our calling to follow Christ.

To follow Christ is to live a life of adoring love for the Father, a life of serving love for the brethren. It is to enter upon a life of continuing conversion, a life ever devoted to doing the will of the Father. To follow Christ is to live a life of love that is kind and patient, caring and helpful, respectful and responsible—a love for God and men to which everything and every law is subordinated. It is a love that finds expression in justice, honesty and truth.

Along with this, there is a corresponding emphasis on the human person and the human situation. The Incarnation means that God has become man. Hence there is great stress on the immanent presence of God in the human condition. As Jesus comes to us in His humanity, we come to God in our humanity. There is great emphasis on what it means to be human, to be human persons in community, in the world—as seen in the light of God's will to reconcile men to Himself in the humanity of Jesus. Once again, such an approach and emphasis will make quite a difference in our understanding of morality and in our wrestling with particular moral problems.

Finally, there is a strong tendency today to see the world, and men in the world, as evolving—man becoming! God is still the Creator, the Lawgiver, the Judge, but this truth is understood in a new way. God has created the world, but not a "finished" or static world. God has created the world according to a design and set certain limits, but within these limits there is much place for development and evolution. God will judge men, but not in terms of a complete set of minutely detailed and universally applicable laws. God has not computerized our lives. Rather, He has made men intelligent and free, with the capacity for creativity and initiative. More than giving men laws, God has given men a task—to rule and govern the world! It is in terms of his own development, and the development of the world, that man is most deeply responsible to God. In terms of *this* responsibility he will be judged.

Thus the personal responsibility of the individual Christian—responsibility that is much *more* than obeying laws, though it is that too—assumes a very basic place in Christian morality and has very much to do with the way in which particular moral questions are understood and resolved. This is so true that many of the moral theologians today define morality as "the response of the Christian to the call of the Father." This response is the "answer" which the Christian gives by freely and creatively assuming the task God has given him, a task that makes man responsible for his own personal growth and development, and the growth and development of the human community, the world. It is in the very performance of this task that redemption occurs, that God's Kingdom comes. (The place and importance of the Church in all this has been clearly indicated in the document of Vatican II, *The Church in the Modern World*.)

So, in this light, the main direction and emphasis of Christian morality today is: act responsibly. I must follow Christ, I must seek first the Kingdom of God, I must change my mind and heart and believe the Good News. I must listen to the teachings of the Church, the laws of God and men. I must above all love others as Jesus loves me and give my life in the service of the brethren. But in all this I am responsible; I must act responsibly—not just in this or that decision, not just in some situations, not just by obeying some laws. I am responsible for the whole moral order, for all laws, for all humanity, for all human institutions, for the Church and for the world. God has made me responsible. So "responsibility" characterizes my whole stance toward life—toward God, men, myself. Morality is responsibility!

ART AND PHOTO CREDITS